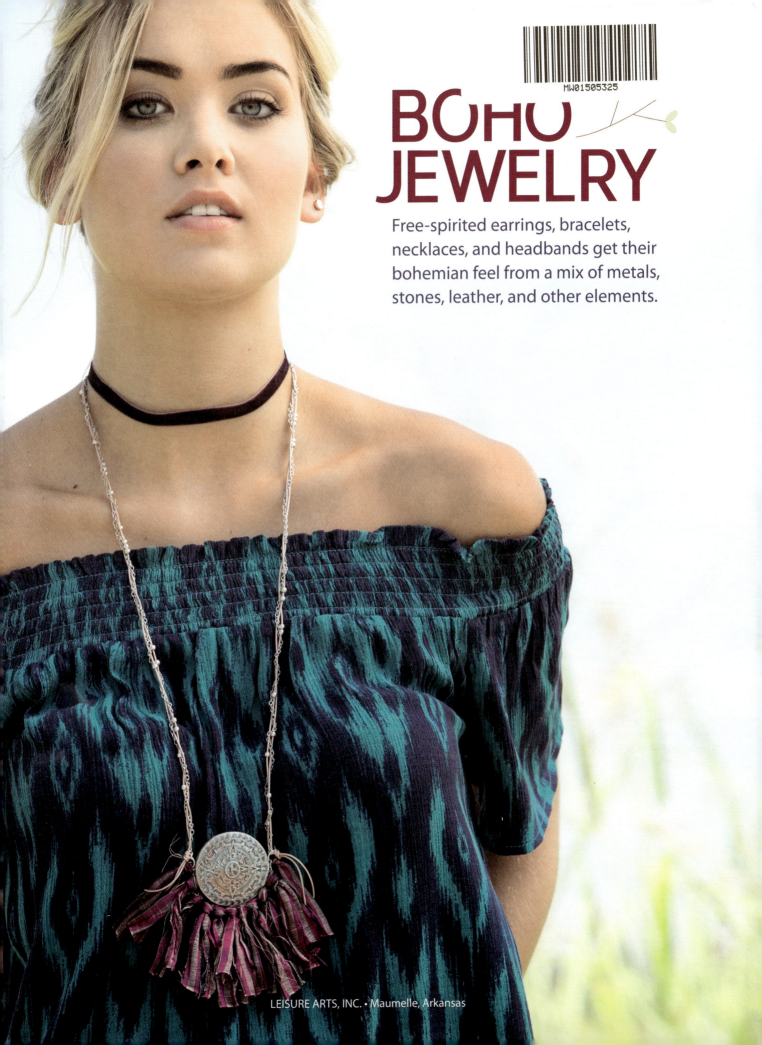

BOHO JEWELRY

Free-spirited earrings, bracelets, necklaces, and headbands get their bohemian feel from a mix of metals, stones, leather, and other elements.

LEISURE ARTS, INC. • Maumelle, Arkansas

CONTENTS

GOLD FLOWER headband

SHOPPING LIST

- ☐ 3 2³⁄₈" diameter gold metal flowers with flat centers
- ☐ 3 ⁷⁄₈" diameter gold/rhinestone shank-style buttons
- ☐ 50" length of gold elastic cord
- ☐ E6000® Industrial Strength Adhesive

To make the Headband:

1. Adhere a button to the center of each flower; allow to dry.

2. Cut 2 elastic lengths that fit comfortably around your head.

3. Thread the elastic lengths through the button shanks. Tie the ends together, adjusting as necessary to fit your head.

VINTAGE BROOCH
bracelet

SHOPPING LIST

- [ ] gold textured leather piece
- [ ] vintage floral brooch
- [ ] 2 $\frac{1}{2}$" diameter buttons for closure
- [ ] sewing needle and thread
- [ ] craft knife
- [ ] E6000® Industrial Strength Adhesive (optional)
- [ ] brown shoe polish and a paper towel (optional)

To make the Bracelet:

1. Cut the leather into a rectangle the desired length and width. I cut mine 7$\frac{1}{2}$" x 1$\frac{7}{8}$". Be sure that your brooch will fit on the leather. If your leather is very shiny, you can rub brown shoe polish on the leather and wipe the excess off with a paper towel.

2. Attach the brooch to the center of the leather strip. You can adhere it permanently to the leather or just pin it around the leather.

3. Sew the buttons to one end of the leather strip. Cut buttonholes at the opposite end of the leather strip.

FLOSS-WRAPPED
earrings

SHOPPING LIST

- ☐ embroidery floss (violet, coral, navy, gold, taupe, and green)
- ☐ 16 10mm x 8mm shell beads in assorted colors
- ☐ 2 silver 1³/₄" long oval hoops with a hole at the top for inserting a head pin
- ☐ 2 silver ear wires
- ☐ 16 6mm silver jump rings
- ☐ 18 silver head pins
- ☐ E6000® Industrial Strength Adhesive

To make each Earring:

See Jewelry Making Basics, pages 21-23.

1. Wrap embroidery floss around an oval hoop, changing colors as desired and using adhesive as necessary.

2. Thread 8 shell beads on 8 head pins; make a loop at the top of each.

3. Use jump rings to attach the shell bead dangles to the hoop.

4. Insert a head pin through the hoop top hole and make a loop. Attach an ear wire to the head pin.

SWAGGED CHAIN
arm bracelet

SHOPPING LIST

- ☐ 24" length of gold very small link chain (I found a chain that had small gold bead links about every 1¹/₄"; this added interest to the chain)
- ☐ 60" length of .5mm leather cord
- ☐ 3 11mm gold/turquoise flat beads
- ☐ 4 14mm x 5mm oval gold links
- ☐ 12 3mm faceted gold beads
- ☐ 18 gold eye pins
- ☐ 4 4mm gold jump rings
- ☐ E6000® Industrial Strength Adhesive
- ☐ 2 pair chain-nose pliers
- ☐ round-nose pliers
- ☐ wire cutters

Adjustable up to 17" circumference

To make the Arm Bracelet:

See Jewelry Making Basics, pages 21-23.

1. Cut two 18" lengths and a 20" length of leather cord. To remove the kinks and bends from the cord, saturate the lengths with water and lay out straight and flat to dry.

2. While the leather cord is drying, cut two 7½" and two 2½" chain lengths.

3. Make 3 connectors by threading gold/turquoise beads on eye pins and making loops at the wire end.

4. Starting with an oval link and alternating with the beaded connectors, join the gold oval links and gold/turquoise beaded connectors.

5. Add a jump ring to each end of a 2½" chain length. Referring to **Photo 1**, use the jump rings to join the 2½" chain length to a 7½" chain length, about 1¾" in from each end. Repeat with the remaining chain lengths.

Fig 1   **Fig 2**

Fig 3

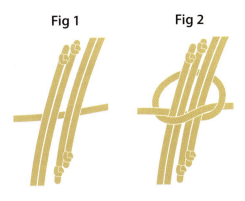

Photo 1

2½" chain length

1¾"   1¾"

Fig 4

6. Referring to **Photo 2**, use the jump rings to join the chain pieces to the bead/link section completed in Step 4.

Photo 2

7. Fold an 18" cord length in half and use a lark's head knot to attach it to an oval link on one end of the bracelet. Repeat to attach the remaining 18" length to the opposite end of the bracelet. Thread 3 faceted gold beads on each cord end. Tie a knot close to the cord end and trim as desired.

8. Arrange the cord ends so that the ends are going in opposite directions. Place the 20" length of cord under the ends *(Fig. 1)*. Refer to **Figs. 2-4** to tie 5 square knots.

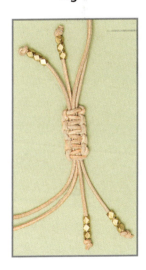

9. Tie a tight knot on the underside of the closure. Apply adhesive to the knot; allow to dry. After the adhesive is dry, trim the cord ends. Apply adhesive to the newly trimmed ends; allow to dry.

10. Loosen the bracelet by gently pulling on the cords. Tighten it by gently pulling on the cord ends.

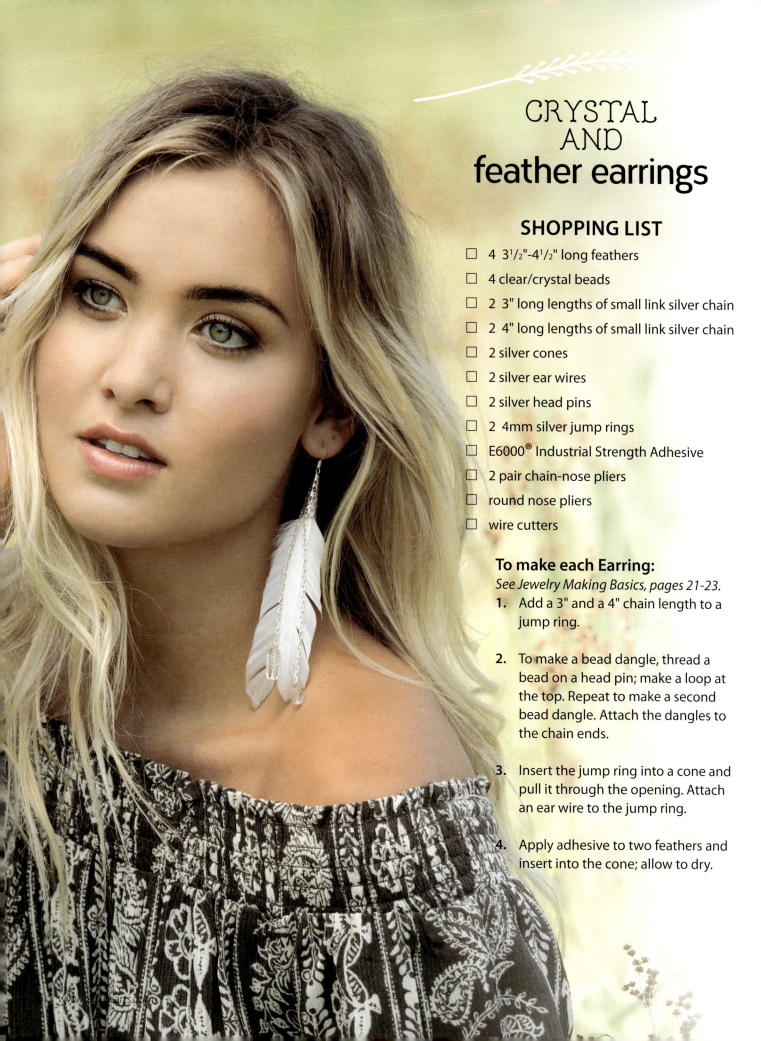

CRYSTAL AND
feather earrings

SHOPPING LIST

- [ ] 4 $3^1/_2$"-$4^1/_2$" long feathers
- [ ] 4 clear/crystal beads
- [ ] 2 3" long lengths of small link silver chain
- [ ] 2 4" long lengths of small link silver chain
- [ ] 2 silver cones
- [ ] 2 silver ear wires
- [ ] 2 silver head pins
- [ ] 2 4mm silver jump rings
- [ ] E6000® Industrial Strength Adhesive
- [ ] 2 pair chain-nose pliers
- [ ] round nose pliers
- [ ] wire cutters

To make each Earring:

See Jewelry Making Basics, pages 21-23.

1. Add a 3" and a 4" chain length to a jump ring.

2. To make a bead dangle, thread a bead on a head pin; make a loop at the top. Repeat to make a second bead dangle. Attach the dangles to the chain ends.

3. Insert the jump ring into a cone and pull it through the opening. Attach an ear wire to the jump ring.

4. Apply adhesive to two feathers and insert into the cone; allow to dry.

TASSELED WRAP bracelet

SHOPPING LIST

- ☐ wax-coated beading cord that will fit through beads
- ☐ large focal bead (I used a 43mm long natural stone bead)
- ☐ small, flat disc beads with large holes (I used 158 5mm beads)
- ☐ ⁵/₈" diameter button
- ☐ two pre-made tassels
- ☐ sewing needle and thread
- ☐ E6000® Industrial Strength Adhesive

To make the Bracelet:

1. Cut a 105" length of beading cord. Fold the cord in half and tie an overhand knot about ³/₄" from the fold. Check to make sure the button will fit in the loop formed.

2. Inserting each cord from opposite sides of the bead, thread a flat bead onto the cords *(Fig. 1)*. Continue to add beads in this manner until the beaded area is about 16" long.

3. Thread the large bead on the cords.

4. Repeat Step 2.

5. Tie the button on the cord ends. Apply a drop of adhesive to the knot; let dry. Trim the cord ends.

6. Hand sew the tassels to the bracelet near the loop knot.

Fig. 1

CRYSTAL POINTS
necklace

SHOPPING LIST

- ☐ 35" length of antique brass medium link chain
- ☐ 27" length of antique brass small link chain
- ☐ 2 crystals (I used quartz points about $5/8$"-$3/4$" long)
- ☐ 48mm x 40mm antique brass oval connector with holes at top and bottom
- ☐ 22mm antique brass ring
- ☐ 24 gauge antique brass jewelry wire
- ☐ antique brass eye pin
- ☐ 4 4mm antique brass jump rings
- ☐ 6mm antique brass jump ring
- ☐ 2 pair chain-nose pliers
- ☐ wire cutters

Finished Length: about 24", without pendant

To make the Necklace:
See Jewelry Making Basics, pages 21-23.

1. Cut a $23^1/2$" length of the medium link chain. Open the link on one end and attach the 22mm antique brass ring; close the link and set aside for now.

2. To make the tassel portion of the pendant, cut a total of ten 3"-$3^1/2$" lengths of both the medium link and small link chains. Make small groups of chain by attaching like lengths together at one end with a 4mm jump ring. Attach the 4mm jump rings to the 6mm jump ring. Trim the eye pin wire to about $3/8$"; make a loop, in the opposite direction, on the eye pin *(Photo 1)*. Join the eye pin to the 6mm jump ring on the tassel.

Photo 1

3. To make the crystal portion of the pendant *(Photo 2)*, insert a 36" length of jewelry wire through one hole in the connector. Wrap the wire around the connector a couple of times and thread the wire through the end link of the $23^1/2$" medium link chain. Wrap the wire around the connector a few more times, securing it in place. Leaving about a $3/8$" space and keeping the wire as tight as possible, wrap the wire around a crystal several times. Leaving just a bit of space, add the remaining crystal in the same manner. Insert the wire through the remaining hole in the connector and wrap the wire around the connector. Thread the wire through the eye pin on the tassel and wrap a few more times. Trim the excess wire and insert the end into the hole or under the wire wraps.

Photo 2

To wear the necklace, pull the long chain through the ring, creating a loop *(Photo 3)*. Slip the loop over your head.

Photo 3

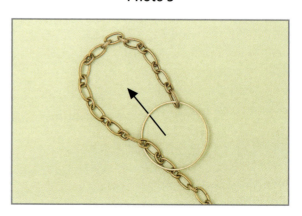

SEED BEAD
earrings

SHOPPING LIST

- ☐ size 15/0 seed beads (light bronze, cream, and peach)
- ☐ 2 pre-made tassels
- ☐ 2 6mm antique gold beads with a large hole
- ☐ 2 antique gold ear wires
- ☐ 4 4mm antique gold jump rings
- ☐ 2 antique gold 2.5mm crimp beads
- ☐ antique gold 7 strand bead stringing wire, no thicker than .30mm/.012 in
- ☐ E6000® Industrial Strength Adhesive
- ☐ 2 pair chain-nose pliers
- ☐ crimp tool
- ☐ wire cutters

To make each Earring:
See Jewelry Making Basics, pages 21-23.

1. Cut 6 6" long wire lengths. Tape one end of all 6 strands (as a group) to your work surface.

2. Slide seed beads on each wire length as follows: 10 light bronze, 10 cream, 20 peach, 10 cream, and 10 light bronze.

3. Thread all 6 wire lengths through a crimp bead. Loop 1 wire length back through the crimp bead *(Fig. 1)*. Pull the wire to make a small loop. Use the crimp tool to secure the crimp bead. Leaving the loop intact, trim the remaining wire ends. Add a drop of adhesive to the wire ends and crimp bead.

Fig. 1

4. Slide a 6mm bead over the wire ends, letting the wire loop extend beyond the bead hole. Use a jump ring to attach an ear wire to the wire loop.

5. Use a jump ring to attach a tassel to one of the beaded wires.

LEATHER WRAP
necklace

SHOPPING LIST

- [ ] 58" length of leather cord
- [ ] large oval bead
- [ ] 4 10mm natural wood beads
- [ ] 2 9mm teal wood disc beads
- [ ] 2 15mm x 7mm green/cream wood beads
- [ ] 2 5mm natural wood beads
- [ ] 88-100 4mm gold jump rings
- [ ] 2 gold eye pins
- [ ] 2 gold head pins
- [ ] 2 9mm gold cord crimps
- [ ] E6000® Industrial Strength Adhesive
- [ ] 2 pair chain-nose pliers
- [ ] round-nose pliers
- [ ] wire cutters

Finished Length: about 60"

To make the Necklace:

See Jewelry Making Basics, pages 21-23.

1. To remove the kinks and bends from the cord, saturate it with water and lay out straight and flat to dry.

2. To make a bead dangle, thread a 5mm wood bead on a head pin and make a loop at the wire end. Repeat with the remaining 5mm wood bead.

3. To make a connector, thread a green/cream wood bead on an eye pin and make a loop at the wire end. Repeat with the remaining green/cream wood bead and two 10mm wood beads to make a total of 4 connectors.

4. Attach a cord crimp to one cord end (*Fig. 1*), placing a drop of adhesive on the cord before closing the crimp over the cord. Join a wood bead connector to the crimp. Join a green/cream bead connector to the wood bead connector and a wood bead dangle to the green/cream bead connector.

Fig. 1

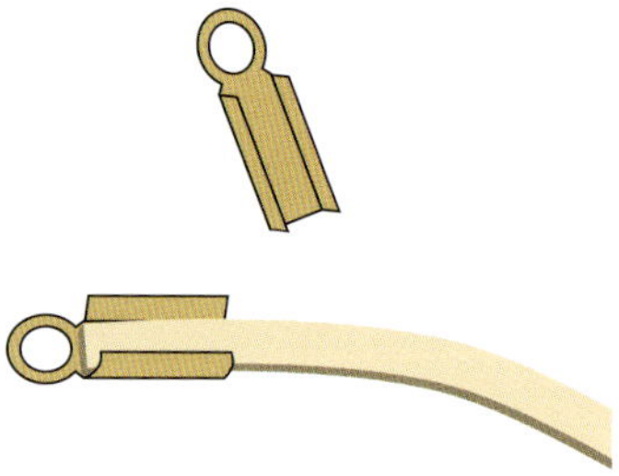

5. Slide 35-40 jump rings on the cord. Slide 3 jump rings, a teal bead, 3 jump rings, a 10mm wood bead, 3 jump rings, the large oval bead, 3 jump rings, a 10mm wood bead, 3 jump rings, a teal bead, and 3 jump rings on the cord; center this grouping on the cord. Apply a drop of adhesive to the outer 3 jump rings on either side to keep them in place. Allow to dry.

6. Slide 35-40 jump rings on the cord. Repeat Step 4 to complete the necklace.

BONE FEATHER necklace

SHOPPING LIST

- ☐ 37" length of antique gold medium link chain
- ☐ 7 antique gold metal teardrop-shaped tags
- ☐ 2 13mm antique gold rings
- ☐ leather cord
- ☐ 2 4" long bone feathers with hole at top
- ☐ 2 antique gold beads (be sure 3 strands of leather cord will fit through each bead)
- ☐ antique gold S-clasp
- ☐ 8 4mm antique gold jump rings
- ☐ E6000® Industrial Strength Adhesive
- ☐ 2 pair chain-nose pliers

Finished Length: about 17$\frac{1}{2}$"

To make the Necklace:

See Jewelry Making Basics, pages 21-23.

1. Cut two 13" lengths of leather cord. To remove the kinks and bends from the cord, saturate the lengths with water and lay out straight and flat to dry.

2. While the leather cord is drying, cut the following chain lengths: one 16$\frac{3}{4}$", one 6$\frac{3}{4}$", and two 4$\frac{1}{2}$" lengths. Open the end link on a 4$\frac{1}{2}$" chain length and attach to a 13mm ring; close the link. Repeat with the remaining 4$\frac{1}{2}$" chain length and 13mm ring. Use a jump ring to attach the clasp to the remaining end of one 4$\frac{1}{2}$" chain length.

3. Use jump rings to attach the tags to the 6$\frac{3}{4}$" chain length, centering one tag and spacing the others evenly toward the ends. Be sure to keep a few chain links free on the ends. Open the end links on the chain length and attach to 13mm rings; close the links.

4. Open the end links on the remaining chain length and attach the ends to the 13mm rings; close the links.

5. Fold each leather cord length in half and attach to a 13mm ring with a lark's head knot.

6. Thread a bead on one set of cords. Slide one cord through the hole in a bone feather. Bend the cord up *(Fig. 1)* and insert it into the bead. Add some glue in the bead hole. Trim the loose cord end even with the bead.

Fig. 1

FRINGED PENDANT
necklace

SHOPPING LIST

- ☐ 42mm ceramic bead
- ☐ 44 3mm silver beads
- ☐ 1/2" x 6" torn strips of silk fabric (I used 11 strips)
- ☐ natural color leather cord
- ☐ 38" length of silver small link chain

- ☐ 4 8mm silver jump rings
- ☐ 4 4mm silver jump rings
- ☐ silver lobster clasp
- ☐ 20 gauge silver jewelry wire
- ☐ 2 pair chain-nose pliers
- ☐ round-nose pliers
- ☐ wire cutters

Finished Length: about 35", excluding fringe

To make the Necklace:

See Jewelry Making Basics, pages 21-23.

1. Cut a 21" length of cord; cut a 16" length of chain. Fold the cord in half and attach to an 8mm jump ring with a lark's head knot. Use a 4mm jump ring to attach the chain end to the 8mm jump ring.

2. Slide about 11 silver beads on each cord. Braid the cords and chain for 15 1/2". Use a 4mm jump ring to attach the chain to an 8mm jump ring. Tie an overhand knot to attach the cord to the same 8mm jump ring. Trim the cord ends to 1 1/2".

3. Repeat Steps 1-2 to make the opposite side of necklace. Attach the clasp to one 8mm jump ring.

4. To make an eye pin for the ceramic bead, cut a 3" wire length. Make a loop on one wire end and slide the bead on the wire. Make a loop on the remaining wire end.

5. Cut a 3" length of chain. Use 4mm jump rings to attach the chain to the eye pin loops on the ceramic bead, allowing the chain to hang beneath the bead. Attach the 8mm jump rings on the necklace to same eye pin loops.

6. Use a lark's head knot to attach each fabric strip to the hanging chain below the bead.

BANDANNA
headband/choker

SHOPPING LIST

- [ ] bandanna
- [ ] rhinestone accent/connector pieces (I used 4)
- [ ] $3/8"$-$5/8"$ wide fusible web tape
- [ ] sewing needle and thread
- [ ] iron
- [ ] E6000® Industrial Strength Adhesive

To make the Headband/Choker:

1. Press the bandanna to remove any wrinkles or creases. Fold the bandanna in half diagonally to make a triangle. Trim away about 3" from the triangle point *(Fig. 1)*; this reduces the bulk when folded.

Fig. 1

3"

2. Starting at the cut end, fold the bandanna into a narrow strip, about 1"-1^1/$_2$" wide. Insert pieces of fusible web tape between the layers and follow the manufacturer's instructions to fuse the layers together.

3. Adhere the rhinestone pieces to the bandanna as desired; allow to dry. Tack each piece to the bandanna in a few places.

Jewelry Making Basics

TOOLS & HOW TO USE THEM

Chain-nose pliers have rounded, tapered jaws and a flat interior surface that will not mar wire or metal findings. These pliers are used for reaching into tight places, gripping objects, opening and closing jump rings, and bending wire. They may also be called needle-nose pliers. You'll need 2 pair to open jump rings and loops on head pins and eye pins.

Round-nose pliers have round jaws that are useful for making loops and bending wire smoothly.

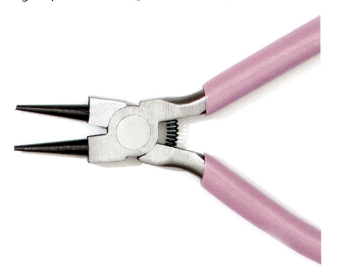

Wire cutters are used to cut beading or small gauge wire, head pins, and eye pins.

A **crimp tool** (also known as crimping pliers) flattens and shapes the crimp bead or crimp tube.

BASIC TECHNIQUES

Making Loops on Head Pins, Eye Pins, or Wire Ends

Slide your beads on a head pin. Leaving about $1/2$", cut off the excess wire. If you are making a large loop, leave more wire at the end.

Using the chain-nose pliers, bend the wire at a 90° angle *(Fig. 1)*. Grasp the wire end with the round-nose pliers. Turn the pliers and bend the wire into a loop *(Figs. 2-3)*. Release the pliers. Straighten or twist the loop further if necessary.

Loops may also be made on eye pins or wire ends the same way.

Opening and Closing Jump Rings and Loops on Head Pins or Eye Pins

Whether you need to attach a clasp, charm, dangle, or other jewelry component, you'll probably use jump rings. Here's how to properly open and close them.

Pick up a jump ring with chain-nose pliers. With a second pair of chain-nose pliers, gently hold the other side of the ring. Open the ring by pulling one pair of pliers toward you while pushing the other away *(Fig. 4)*.

Fig. 1

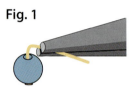

Fig. 2

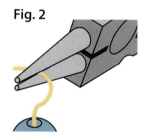

Fig. 3

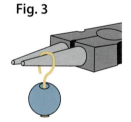

Fig. 4

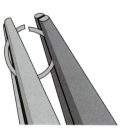

Close the ring by pushing and pulling the pliers in opposite directions, bringing the ring ends back together.

You'll open and close chain links and the loops on head pins and eye pins the same way.

Using Crimp Beads or Tubes

To finish a wire end, thread a crimp bead or tube and the clasp or jump ring on the wire. Run the wire back through the crimp bead; use a pair of pliers to pull and tighten the wire *(Fig. 5)*. Place the crimp bead or tube on the inner groove of the crimp tool and squeeze *(Fig. 6)*.

Fig. 5

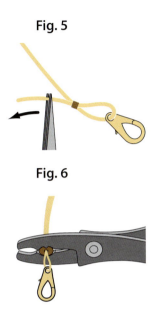

Fig. 6

Release the tool, turn the crimp bead or tube a quarter turn, and place it in the outer groove *(Fig. 7)*. Squeeze the tool to round out the crimp bead or tube *(Fig. 8)*. Trim the wire end or if the design calls for beads, thread the beads over the wire to cover the end.

Fig. 7

Fig. 8

Overhand Knot

Tie an **overhand knot** with cords, suede cords, or ribbon *(Fig. 9)*.

Fig. 9

Lark's Head Knot

Fold the cord in half. Place the loop through the ring, link, or clasp. Bring the cord ends through the loop and pull to tighten *(Fig. 10)*.

Fig. 10

MEET LORI WENGER

"I've always been a designer of some form or fashion," says Lori Wenger. "And when the opportunity arose for me to design jewelry, I took it on as a new exciting challenge!"

Lori was a Leisure Arts staff designer for more than seven years, contributing to books in The Spirit of Christmas and Gooseberry Patch series, among others. Since 2012, she has been a contributing photostylist for numerous Leisure Arts publications.

"My freelance career allows me to work in many different creative genres, from the photo styling, to illustrating, to designing. And luckily I have the continued support of a loving husband and two beautiful children."

Lori's most recent designs published by Leisure Arts include subtle statement jewelry pieces in Tasseled Jewelry (#7079) and vintage-inspired decorative accessories in Cool String Art (#7164). More of Lori's creations may be found on Instagram: lori_wenger.

We have made every effort to ensure that these instructions are accurate and complete. We cannot, however, be responsible for human error, typographical mistakes, or variations in individual work.

Production Team: Technical Writer – Mary Sullivan Hutcheson; Technical Associates – Lisa Lancaster and Jean Lewis; Editorial Writer – Susan Frantz Wiles; Senior Graphic Artist – Lora Puls; Graphic Artist – Leia Morshedi; Photostylist – Lori Wenger; Photographer – Jason Masters.

Made in U.S.A.